The Clever Daugh

Susan Wicks grew up in Kent and studied French at the universities
of Hull and Sussex, where she wrote a PhD thesis on the fiction of
André Gide. She has taught in France and at University College,
Dublin. She now lives with her husband and two daughters in
Tunbridge Wells, and works as a part-time tutor for the University
of Kent. Her first novel will be published in 1997.

Susan Wicks
The Clever Daughter

faber and faber
LONDON · BOSTON

First published in 1996
by Faber and Faber Limited
3 Queen Square London WC1N 3AU

Photoset by Wilmaset Ltd, Wirral
Printed and bound in Great Britain by Mackays of Chatham PLC, Kent

A CIP record for this book
is availabled from the British Library

ISBN 0-571-17926-6

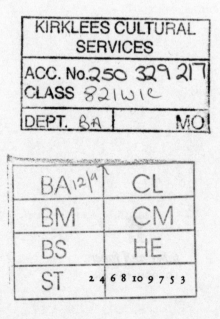

Contents

Acknowledgements

Poems from this collection have appeared in *Ambit, Beloit Poetry Journal* (U.S.A.), *Carolina Quarterly* (U.S.A.), *Grand Street* (U.S.A.), *Independent, London Quarterly, London Review of Books, New Statesman, Partisan Review* (U.S.A.), *Poetry Durham, Poetry Review, Poetry Wales, Prairie Schooner* (U.S.A.), *Rialto, Southern Review* (U.S.A.), *Spectator, Stand, Times Literary Supplement, Writing Women.*

I should like to thank the Ragdale Foundation and the Virginia Center for the Creative Arts, where a number of these poems were written.

s.w.

Rain Dance

This is how they make rain, the raw
repeated drumbeat of two pulses, this green gauze
that settles on their skin and gleams
like light on water. This is how he creates her,
fluid as green drops fusing
on new growth, bent to this holy posture
of damage, her raised green satin instep
stroking her own right cheek, as he still turns her,
twists her as if through creepers,
this green sediment of branches
layered on air, as his taut body
dances on hers. They will reach the light soon. He bends her
this way and that, her head flips backwards
into his darkness, her neck surely broken.
Her two legs split perfectly open
like roots. There is moisture
between them now as he drags her, wood
rasping her inside thighs. The rapt watchers
gasp with her pain, if she could only
feel it. Curved for his blessing,
her skin glistens as he still strokes her
like a green pot into being
on this wheel of rhythms
where they are gods, unmindful now of bodies,
our single-jointed history
of breakage, and the sweat runs off them.

Drums

Hearing the drum-beat, I have
come to you. Your boy-shadow
tortures the rusting oil-drums
in the clearing: as they buckle
the wombs of stale air throb,
the birds fly up, startled. At my feet
wild anemones glitter, a forked path
leads to these echoes. In this space
you test me: I must balance
on the thinnest of branches
to become one of you,
as the long call moves on, wraps us
in silence. The spotted foxgloves
close in, the branch is furred with moss.
A drop of rusty water continues
to vibrate, our drum corroding
to lace. We are detached now
as leaves; we fall slowly,
grow intricate and brittle
at our white edges, lie
together. The warm muzzles
of starving creatures come to us,
sniff at us, turn our bodies over,
forage for scents in our buried goodness.

Repos de Noce

Our marriage has come of age. You greet me
with a painted wedding-breakfast
under low branches, faces flushed with drink,
a white carnation on a black lapel, the bow-ties
of sunburned Norman peasants, this crumpled napkin
trailing to grass. Here is our young girl leaning
to torment flowers, here are our blown roses
in a vase, our side of beef, expensive juices
bleeding from the centre, as the bride
clinks glasses with that white-draped figure
raising his wine like poison, or a child
presented in a shawl, a hole
where his hand should be. And in the distance,
where the dark arm reaches,
the deep pools of trees, the sun
hazed with summer dust, an old wall
dappled as if with first blossom.

Components of Black

for Cathleen Daly
(watercolour, 40" × 60")

In clutches of pale eggs, or the bone china
of raised tea-cups, the simple snow of paper
gleams from between shadows all shades but
black: grey, green-blue, violet, that old indigo
across eyelids, the dark chromatic beds
of night rivers. See how this multiple darkness
pushes plump leaves aside to wind
between stems, how this slick beanstalk
has grown to block the daylight, how the tangled
limbs bruise to slate, bronze to a warm olive
shot with purple, before the chosen
stems can wilt, the pale mouths of camellias
gag open, damned to repeat for us
our eyes' clear grain, our painted jungle
of pigment, the darkness between flowers.

Human Geometry

The soft line of her arm
extends under the table, her hand touches

his knee. Somewhere outside perception
the planes of their two bodies

come together. Later in warm darkness
I represent them, their two forms congruent

under stars, their eyes closed, speaking
no shared language. I hear them,

the hiss of their late-night shower
on the tiled wall, their urine

running in the bowl, her precise footsteps.
I trace her conjectural return

to a segment of shared circle
labelled with letters, her chord of voices

rising like children's, the arc of his body
melting on hers like a solution.

Room of His Own

You can tell his wife has left him, from books
and letters that slide on each surface, the paper
in the shower shredding to mildew, the stark
pupating clothes-line, folded for winter.

These are her dust-motes floating over a chair
to suck up sun, her framed daughter
caught in a net of light, her fine hair
lifted on deep grass from another era.

What he has is a view over trees, a few things
that are his, a drift of bills in the hall
to trip him as he turns his recalcitrant key

in the lock: this long room where he can be
himself, his posters curled on the wall,
shirts clinging to banisters like damp wings.

Three-quarter Cello

His brown-gold hair is slippery
as a child's, his slit eyes almost
shut as if for laughter. His soft arm
moves over the grain, pauses,
pulls notes from the wooden body
as the old music rises
almost true, his new three-quarter
voice calling for answers.

There is no answer to this
mouth, this arm, this concentration
of breathing. My own eyes narrow
to slits. My own body
shudders, the discrete notes almost
fuse to a phrase, a lost concert
of voices, childlike, studious –
true as we could make them.

My Daughter at Kilpeck

Beyond this small church, my daughter
stands on a green lip, her back
straight and still, her hair lifted
against corn-stubble, the grey uncertain
weather of late summer. Slowly I circle
one last time, look up to study
the stuck corbels – boar, ram, lion,
dog and rabbit – their eyes still watching
for the stone huntsman, as above me his woman,
cold clinch of knees and elbows,
yanks her stone slit open
as if for blood. I slip back into the dark
between carved folds, and see my daughter
still in the same green place
while over us the sharp creature
face erodes, a slow strand of hillside
probes her like moist silk
and moves on, through her stone lips
into harvest, the eye of her needle.

Landing

We meet on landings: outside the night
is furred with frost. You are warm,
sleepy as fruit, your peach satin
pyjamas rumpled, scented with breath.

Below us an old house
hums. Through windows the dark
is a net of trees, trapped stars.
Darling, in the cold airways

a woman flares in a reek of petrol,
children murder children with bricks. Bodies
such as yours lie buckled, blackened
on hard shoulders. Sleepless,

I meet you, we cling to each other,
our hearts beat back gravity, feathered
in red juice like a split stone.

Your Baby

We were the ones who stole her,
took her from her pram unwitnessed,
peeled the damp clothes from her body.

We stroked her cheek raw with love,
combed out her rasp of tangles
to red silk, kept her nails in a casket.

We washed her soft creases, lulled her
with the pressure of fingers, wrapped her
in leaves. We knelt to feed her

to the dark. Now in this sunlit corridor
your thin breasts sag as you still cradle
an old doll. The synthetic features

worry your flesh, the tufted
hair stands out with longing. *Have you seen
my baby?* And we must answer

for this hard grey skin, these nails
perfect as shells, these ball-and-socket
limbs, this plastic slit

mouth that is beyond telling.

Fox

The evening my mother died we first saw
its face – fur, a moment's meeting
of eyes, a quick ripple from the path
into undergrowth. Over us, the green reaching
of birch and beech, the new tangle
of wild honeysuckle. And repeating,
that one cuckoo, its measured heartbeat
across grass and bluebells. Then a second time,
rounding a blind bend, the brush lifted
on a ground of sunlight, seeming to give us
darkness, the spine seeming to open
a new space hidden between tree-trunks,
the gap that would let it slip to earth again,
the tight bracken masking it over.

Understairs

This is where you would hide
from your own mother
as she screamed and ranted
till they came to take her:
cobwebs across faces,
gas-pipes, inscrutable pointers,
the old mop with its grey head
leaning. Knotted rags
hang by the half-closed
boxes of turning apples.
On a ripple of dust and cider
your empty wicker basket
rocks, discovered. Daughters,
we huddle together, hands
to our mouths, stopping
the high voices.

Caves

I would not make you enter
the caves, the cleft face
where saplings hang by knotted
hair-roots. I would not ever take you
in through the dark passages,
their mineral growth closing
on lit white pools,
basins pitted with slow water,
this hollow matrix of footprints.
I would not take you in
to where our own breathing
pushes us both towards daylight,
your screams slaked in lime, the fat
droplets welling to completion.
I would leave you to wait patiently
in the circle of grey air above me
as I went down to visit,
following the roped causeway,
the stars looping back through darkness
to where you still are, sitting
in summer grass, grateful
you are not asked to go with me.

Persephone

Wanting someone who looked natural,
they cast you as Persephone, not thinking
how at regular intervals you were taken
to visit your own mother
under a flaking sky of cream paint
down the echoing corridor
to the long-stay ward, where trees
froze in the black glass
of winter – how you were no stranger
to the clockwork rhythms of figures
moaning and swaying, the mechanical
hands that moved across faces
or scattered things in odd corners,
the hungry hands that flapped after
with their wings of ragged knitting.
Each time you would leave her and return
to birdsong, the urgent green
through frost, the melting grass, the world
you would give her if she would only
recognise you through the heavy doors
your father closed between you. Each week
you rehearsed your flower-steps
with a basket of paper petals
as your teachers smiled down on you, exclaiming
at your sweet face,
at the way you seemed never to see him coming –
as if each last dance were the first dance,
and every mother won over by so little.

Grandmother

These were my mother's: against a window
of trees, sky, sunlight, I fill sacks
with intimate things, tear up, pull down,
straighten my aching back. Here are
the home-made pyjama trousers
with no jackets, the wilting knickers,
the corset she bought and could never quite
squeeze herself into. Her old soft
working-dresses cling to me. Here is
the long escaping coil of child's hair
in its hood of crumpled paper, the letter
about the French kissing, the photograph
of myself at eight, eyes clear and
watchful, the little covered basket
of soaps, the handkerchiefs embroidered
in foreign countries. And in a dark box
where the painted birds flutter,
my father's one last tooth, yellowed,
long as a wild animal's, gleaming
between the frayed silk scarves,
the lacy night-things of a grandmother.

Flames

This is the black and white photograph
that I shall burn first, my young mother
in the wind at Margate,
self-conscious and smiling as the child
pulls back and away from her
and sulks, the silver-paper glitter of kite-tail
still streaming. These are the
flames, the crackling red and orange,
the hungry black ring that moves outwards.
And this one, with my father
standing on a mound to reach up
another two inches, as she looks laughing
over canal, trees, valley, the Dijon summer
colours disappearing in a stroke
of rising light, the transparent centre.
Or this one, taken much later,
the two of you always together,
against bulb-fields blazing
with red tulips, that I shall
leave until last, that perhaps I will not need
even to put a match to.

Bubbles

A microwave has replaced my mother.
We divide its clear wrapping between us
with scissors, letting our fingers travel
over the fat blisters, remembering
the bladder-wrack of our lost summers,
a slippery harvest of rank gases.

Climbing the stairs I hear it
rising at our heels, the frantic crackle
of four bare soles as my daughters
dance on air, the multiple small explosion
of crushed cells from Atlantis.

Buried in her things I found a picture
of bubbles, drawn in my childhood,
the bright circles crowding up to heaven
with primitive passion, my own
oh dear one's poped, trying
to describe departure.

Listen with Mother

Only this: an old armchair,
a sideboard, sun on carpet;
time, and the child
uncurls, strokes the warm
dog sleeping, dances
to find her mother. She can
hear her, the sweet small
chink of glass in the kitchen,
a tap running. No need
to listen, she will always
dance from the chair,
the old dog will always
be sleeping. On tiptoe
she is skipping
across carpet towards her
busy music of absence, the
clash of crockery, the cold tap's
gurgle rising and falling.

Blind Date

Among the tables and steel teapots
I thought I was meeting a stranger.

A pot of tea for us, a miracle,
your hand raising and raising it.

The same rain on our two faces
as we talk of the same lost lover.

Now that you are dead, I find
our two griefs are compatible.

Cloud Parting

As we climb, clouds
peel like skin under us,
leave us smaller and needy:
soft flesh, gums, reflexes.

The tatters part and gather,
give us these new shapes:
a handful of hair streaming,
the multiple red eyes of a city.

Whatever is left of you, whatever
still lies over slate and brick,
is churned in our updraught,
fans out now to a ripple.

Our ascent has buried you
in air, stars. Skyscrapers
push deep into earth, their long roots
reach up to suck on you.

Dispersal

My mother is dispersed. The open window
admits her body.

The soapy water turns, retains the shape
of her rough finger;

the steam from the runner beans displaces her
only slightly.

I fill my lungs with her, hold, expel her gently
into sunlight.

The grass under the apple-tree pushes up into her.
A creeping wasp

buries itself deep in her dark places.

On Re-recording Mozart

When the throb of her voice was cut off, I drove
through streets white with silence: no sound
but my own engine, as if above or beyond
the gear-change a knife glittered, and love

itself were cut out, its high vibrating tongue
docked with a neat flick as the full reel
still turned, clicking, lashing its little tail
at nothing, and silence became her whole song.

Now I have re-recorded Mozart, my tape
unwinding across chasms. Between one note
and the next she still breathes. Her breath

pulls me across darkness, the last escape
of bodies. Rising from her new throat
it redeems and redeems us. I have erased death.

Mute Swans

In the still evening two swans,
twin ghosts across black water,
glide closer and the two beaks
merge, the stretched pale necks fuse
to a perfect heart, squeezed ever tighter
until the dark centre
fills, the last gleaming feather
dies in the curve of the bodies'
slow shrinkage to a half-remembered
mouth, a hat, a white bow floating
on deep water.

              But no, they have
passed each other, they separate,
they have vacated the night's mirror,
that last light from the sky,
the symmetry
that made disappearance necessary.

Weir

You died long ago and the trees
in the river are thin copper
beaten to sunlight. In moving water
our world is precious as wreckage,
its sunken carcass rolled and
remade; the impact of a drop
rings us like deep treasure.

This is where time slides open
on a sheet of sky, as the churned bodies
of trunks rise for ever, bare
a gleam of white shoulders.

Below the barrier
circles widen, drift eastwards
like green footprints.

Knot

Let me do to you what they do
to the dead – now, while you are still
alive, your blank moon face hanging
half-empty, as if begging.

Let me wash and fill you
with soft white stuff, feed cotton
into your loose cheeks, gather
your jaw shut with silk chiffon.

Let me do it to you now,
paint my cosmetic sunset
across your cheekbones, comfort
your tired eyelids with pennies.

Later, when you die, we can
cut through silk, let the face fly
open, the scarf shake out
its map of escaping creases, as we

roll wet swabs between us
like picnic eggs, the familiar
bag flapping, the small change
jingling again in our purses.

After the Tornado

We have entered your own country
of disasters. The candlelight
gives us all death's-heads, yellow

as ripe cheeses. We eat and laugh
with the living, but we listen
for the silence of a darkened world

that has stopped breathing. Casually
we catch drips, empty buckets,
mop surfaces. Through the man-sized hole

where roof should be the stars
move in. By the smoky flicker
I fill our five plates, pour wine, we even

clink glasses. At last I see you
smile. You are king here. Our dust
settles on your thin crown like kisses.

Midas

You touch grass with your fingertip
and it goes grey, the sky is weighted.
Trees turn to metal as you
breathe on them, the small birds
dropping from their branches
like dull ornaments. My mother's clock
has stopped. A warm mouthful
hardens to lead in your gullet.
Your limbs' own inertia
drags you from the step, your stick
a stiff snake dead under your knuckles.

This is what you wished for, this
has been granted. Your precious daughter
is starting to resemble you.
The whole world swings out
and comes to rest
taut and true as a plumb-line
from your extended finger.

Hans Andersen Plays with Shadows

He might almost have created this
himself, with patience and small scissors:
the split trunk of an old cedar,
twigs spilling in a black fountain.

He could surely have snipped out
these squirrels, their dark bush-tails spreading
in mid-leap, the bunch and stretch of muscle
translated to flatness, shapes pressed on sunset.

His sharp hand might even have added
a corpse hanging from the lower branches,
its twin delicately unfolding
in a crinkle of serrated edges –

enough to make him start shaking
with fear for his intricate creation,
in this world of red-hot skies and bodies
cut loose, worming, so much burnt paper.

My Father is Shrinking

When we last hugged each other
in the garage,
our two heads were level.
Over his shoulder I could see
potato-sacks.

Another season
and in the dusty sunlight
I shall gather him to me,
smooth his collar,
bend to listen
for his precious breathing.

When he reaches
to my waist,
I shall no longer
detach his small hands
from my skirt,
escape his shrill voice
in the dawn garden.

When he comes to my knees,
I shall pick him up and rock him,
rub my face on the white
stubble of his cheek,
see his silver skull
gleam up at me
through thin combings.

My Father's Handkerchiefs

In a controlled explosion
of dry grief, fragile as skeletons,
trembling in my hand like my daughter's
origami monsters, their worn muslin
stiff with mucus, they let me prise them
open. With a sound like tearing
the crumbs of snot flick out at me,
my father's latest creations
dead. Each week I wash them,
press warmth into the yielding creases
and bring them back – so many
neat flat squares for him
to snort his thick grief into. Each week
I find them again, wreckage
of crippled beasts and flowers
to flutter or creep or scuttle
into my machine
as I try to name them: butterfly,
tortoise, crane, crab, lily,
cygnet, crane, crane, crane, crane.

Airborne

*The navigator will have considerable difficulty at
first in determining the direction of waves far
below him. By looking down as nearly vertically
as possible and concentrating on a single wave
and then another the direction of their
movement should soon become apparent.*

Airborne, we have synchronised
watches. In my lap I study
the grey waves of your handwriting,
your meticulous pencilled isobars,
the paper yellowed and crumbling.
Together we take off. It is wartime.
Stacked over the coast, the clouds already
test us, as we take our first
fixes. Lights flare up to meet us, half-
blind you, age you a half-century
as before birth I limp back,
my small engine coughing,
towards Miami Beach, the swelling coastline
of Florida. Leaving my mother
alone in the rationed darkness,
you surely recognise this ocean,
its wrinkles and grimaces. Together
we look down at seething highways,
at roofs and beaches, as you point out to me
the weather that can swirl across them,
the rucked skin of the Atlantic,
which way the waves are breaking.

Forgotten Light

Today I shall draw back the curtain
on the landing, and see lichen
like mustard on the garage roof, the winter
jasmine in the next garden, a year's clouds
blowing in across the ridge-tiles.
My father's pale green carpet
will be as it once was, before shade
turned it to moss. A drift of hand-prints
will rise on the hall plaster
where he has leaned his weight
all these months, the whorls of his grey fingers
like a sleepy child's in the half-dark. I shall
press my own hands in them,
see how our two spans almost
fit, but not quite. I shall see insects
dance on the warm glass, newly woken.

My Father's Caul

Is this my father's skin
or my grandmother's,
twice folded
in its blue envelope,
like a promise of wings?

I tease it open,
see the intimate creases
whitened and flaking,
see my own fingers
shine through it,
as if my father
floated clear of us,
his skin perfect
and impermeable,
his life melting to wax.

Now this dry moon rises
in cold currents.
The attic shadows
play over it.
I see it falling
through air,
its stretch of membrane
slick with grease,
the purple features
flattened to a gasp,
the new-born
mouth, nose, eyes, fingers
sealed in a bag of skin
and sent back to her,
slippery, anonymous.

First Sleep

My father sleeps now, his head lolling
to one side, mouth gaping, his hollow
face abandoned. Yet his eyes
slide under open lids
like a baby's. Is he dreaming
of mothers, of their soft
flesh against his fist,
their smile lifting into focus,
the breast receding? Is he dreaming
of voices, his dream nothing
but a slit of wet light,
a pond glimpsed between branches?
His slow raft moves over
rank weeds, navigates lilies,
rusting iron bedsteads, the slimy
mouth of an old bottle. Under the surface,
eyes, reflections of eyes. I see him
move his mouth slowly
as if searching.

Protected Species

My parents' papers lie round me
bundled in boxes, the lids dotted
with the droppings of bats, the names
faded, too faint for a stranger's eye
to interpret. I pull, and the perished bands
snap into dust, a grey sheet blisters
with flying fragments. *Joy darling*:
in the roof his circling voice
transmits its high-pitched signal
to her voice. My parents' wartime letters,
starred with small explosions, have flown
great distances, their words blanching
on the page, their steady messages
bringing the world back
to an attic where protected species
hang upside-down, flexing
their claws in a dream of darkness,
shaking their skinny wings.

Leaf-storm

Clearing my father's house, I have room
only for miniatures: his freezer,
its little lid propped open, the thumbnail
meat-safe, three barley-twist tables that nest
in my hand. Cupped in my fingers
my parents' bed lies waiting, a glass-topped
cabinet of remedies, a five-pronged hoe,
tines humbled with rust. Now I can turn them
upside-down, his rootless objects
trapped in the blue glass of October
with the bones of oak, beech,
ash. A gold blizzard
swirls and settles in my palm,
buries them in glitter, in slow leaves.

Pigeons

All eyes and beaks, they travel
to somewhere in Europe. Released
they read the grey Channel like a palm,
follow the dark lifeline northwards
into fog. Breasting pale cliffs
they wheel over the M2, ride
the poison updraught towards
home. What if they home
on nothing, beating in smaller circles
till home comes? Here is the trodden earth
where their shed used to be, its few grains
of rank corn. Here are their drinking-tubes,
cracked open. Here is the statue,
the sunlit ridge-tile
outlined in gold, the tree.

Talisman

Tonight I shall let the train take me
in a long clanking dream of America,
freight shifted from coast to coast,
dark wagons scratched with symbols.

They will carry me to my father
in his country. Dark-suited, in a trilby,
he leans through steam to wave to me,
his furled newspaper brushing the window

while at the far point of the garden
the child stands watching, goldenrod
bursting on her head as the red spiders
blister the fence like rust, where

adders lie sleeping. This is her penny,
thin as a new leaf, its veins
beaten in bright metal, where the wheels bit,
his old face gone, clean now as a whistle.

The Clever Daughter

after a misericord in Worcester Cathedral

For six hundred years I have travelled
to meet my father. *Neither walking nor riding*,
I have carried your heartbeat to him
carefully, to the sound of singing,
my right hand growing to horn.

Your head droops in a stain of windows
as we come closer. The man who made us —
hare and girl — will barely recognise
the lines his blade left: six centuries
have fused us to a single figure.

Clothed and unclothed, we shall reach him,
netted at his cold feet. But as he unwraps us,
my cloak-threads snagging and breaking,
I shall release you, your pent flutter
of madness. And we shall see you

run from his hands and vanish,
your new zigzag opening the cornfield
like the path of lovers, the endless journey
shaken from your long ears, my gift to him
given and yet not given.

Green

How can we live with green,
this ache of trees, this perennial reaching
into light, the air that dances?

We have stood in this place so long
our feet are thirsty, our skin is crumbling
bark, we host insects. Still

these lifting branches wave to us
as if casually, move closer, flesh out
the gaunt hillside. Each May

I rock with my green loves, my dressed
skeletons. Their whispers
pull me from sleep like a baby.

Spring

We have left our faces in the puddles
with the silver edges of clouds half-buried
in water, twigs all reaching down to the centre
of the earth for light, the small birds
hopping and fluttering deeper and deeper
into silt – our silvered faces
trapped by the downward-seeking branches
on clear blue, the glint of high planes,
vapour-trails wrapping us with white ribbons.

Soar Mill Cove

For now the sand holds
the print of feet: an old film
whirrs in slow motion

without burning. These boys
are any small boys, on tiptoe
across shingle, their shoulders

jutting like wings. Settled
behind wind-breaks, our mothers
click their squares of short needles,

re-footing last year's socks; the father
stands with his camera to catch
a son's grin, his perfunctory

peck on barnacled rock,
the girl recoiling. Now they will
kiss until the film melts. Watch

how they repeat us,
how we start to shine, backlit,
as we drop from the frame like stitches.

Burgh Island, 1st September

I could stand here all night watching
the tide come in, where unknown children
squeal as the sea wraps them
in cold, and the next wave crawls towards us,
wriggles into footprints. I could
begin to admire God,
His repeats and ritual hesitations,
the lace of brown scum His slow fingers
have ravelled, His sliced shells and pebbles
in subtle calibrations as the sea stirs them
and leaves them, a moated castle
levelled to a streak. All night I could stand holding
the straps of my flapping sandals
till the land was a cold stroke in darkness
and the strait opened to my bare feet
in running furrows, the one causeway
narrowed to a spine of ripples
and the Island, its hotel, its sharp grasses,
cut off – till the sea tractor
lumbered out again to its harvest of water.

Starehole Bay Sphinx

I stare at rocks and see
no answer, the old paws
clenched on spray, the haunches
furred with bracken, tawny gorse.
As if blown here,
this desert creature crouches,
the head severed,
knuckles still clutching
at low water, the body
discrete and predatory. I will not
tell it what I know, I will not
throw down the mauled syllable.
It waits. The one eye
opens on air. A cloud
floats up like an iris. Below us
the waves break, gleam, whisper
What animal, what animal?

Jocasta's Gift

Let me tell you what I have saved for you:
my wise hands, the years of whispers,
an old shadow rippling across desert,
the cave-mouth echoing with jackals.

Your scarred footprints lie drying on marble
as dawn washes the standing columns.
You sleep perfectly at my dark nipple,
my strong scarf twisted, heavy with water.

It was a good storm, it is a very clean city
in the rags of its surviving palm-trees.
The ruins begin to outlive us.

But I have saved you your mother's body,
her red brooch dripping into darkness,
the night voices of all our waking children.

Changeling

You were the unborn son, the wizened brother
my daughters would never know.
Like a yolk you were scraped out of me.

Now you return, rocking at my fireside
in the grey arms of smoke, your cracked laughter
shaking the eggshells, as the steam rises

from your skin. Your eyes start open
and the cupped water boils on my hearth:
this fragile membrane contains hunger.

Soon I shall hear singing
high in the chimney. My own face
mouths at me, wrinkled

to the likeness of a stranger.
Welcome. I see you are the baby
born easily, the one my breasts fill for.

Device

Rampant on red, stark as a small scarecrow
on a ground of sunsets,
it spreads its two limbs

in warning. Far off, in the deep furrows
the life still ripens, bursts, bleeds
to nothing as the inner weather

still changes, washes
the outstretched arms in a sudden flood
of colour. It is evening. Now the horizons

are fading. The silver flocks
rise up and up. A last gleam
plays on copper like September lightning.

Three Tales

after Flaubert

1

You are the butcher saint: the mouse
bleeding on cold stone, the sleepy
birds chopped from branches
still ring you with longing – the stag,
the fawn slaughtered with the mother.
No wonder your own parents
lay in your marriage-bed, as if resting
from unnatural acts, no wonder the stranger
called you from across the river
to ferry him in death's own weather,
then wrapped you with his old man's body,
his sores embroidering you like cloth, your skin
clothing him, your hermit's hovel
split from ear to ear, your poor roof
flying wide open, as you
became stained glass.

2

She is the consummate dancer,
her grey silk shadow on marble
as her scorpion body arches
its fountain of piercing juices.
From the floor she can almost see it,
the grey-faced prophet's sneer
from the pit, the hungry trophy
hauled between them for centuries
across desert, crying its dead message.

Before them she still dances; she knows
she is beautiful, that heaven
and Herod jump to her rhythms,
her bent spine, her eyebrows black
as wingtips; and she dances
for the ruler with his poor hunger,
for the glutton puking under the table,
for her mother, for her life; and she pictures
a man's head on a platter – what else
should she ask for?

3

Here is the makeshift altar
set up in a back courtyard,
her flowers and jumbled objects,
her glassy moth-eaten treasure
and these its loveliest feathers,
that patch of surviving wing-silk
like sky spread there under her,
loud with the pulsing heat-haze
as she dies –
blue as unmapped countries,
beady with bright languages,
screeching the mimic diction
of the Holy Ghost,
settling on her shoulder and clawing
at her nightgown
like a lover, a lost child,
her own heart.

Monet: The Chicago Haystacks

It has taken us years to create
this palimpsest: haystacks pregnant with light,
these shadow-skirts belling
towards onlookers. Now we have surrendered
our coats, our back-packs, our tweed
headgear. Our necks no longer remember
zips, the snap collars of down jackets:
now there is nothing between us
but a plastic chip. Your fruit-shimmer
becomes our breathing, your snow
melts for us; your sharp stalks
write on our cold faces. In layers of light
the mottled stack reclothes itself.
Our eyes blink back ghosts, our fingers close
on air. Leaving our shuttered lenses,
our Walkmans' coiled umbilicals
of flex, our shiny packages, we have reached
into light, snow, haystacks. Our bare hands
rifle you, topple your ricks
with inept strokes, as we roll together
in interior dark. We look at you. We shimmer
with death, rose, winter, peeling you
to see one another.

May Dogwoods

From the matted crannies
of ravines, their wings flutter
in pale flocks, gleam like relics
of frost. Up tangled hillsides,
through the close sweat of valleys,
I follow the trail of flowers
to its end, this intimate meeting
of white on pink, each delicate centre
pinned on clear ether. My path dissolves,
winds into silence, woods settle
over woods, wings on wings –
the high crowns of trees
slow-dance like church-spires.
He comes at me, his tight-knotted
sneakers slung across one shoulder,
close-clipped head gleaming
through dark froth, his skin smooth
as iced coffee, grins,
'Hi.' Light glances,
picks out his roadside shack,
its blue tin roof;
the road we walk on
shimmers like water.
'Hi,' I say. 'Hi. Hi.'

Joy

The authorities do not permit us
to take pictures: this dance is ephemeral
as sex or April dogwoods, the pink-skirted
ripple of her body, her emaciated
trunk gleaming, the snapped wishbone
of her thigh sparking light. The pink wit
of her flexed foot stirs us unaccountably
to laughter. This is the dancer's way, this meeting
of tangent bodies, this cool coffee
at café tables, the momentary pink stasis
of words, the fading blossom
drifted from chestnuts. This must be spring,
her limbs' own joy, as his arms lift her,
carry her on his shoulders
into darkness. We may not take pictures.
We look and look, drinking
the small death of each step, each contact
of flesh on sliding flesh, the precise circles
of what we crave, the gasps that express us.